BROKEN HALLELU*J*AHS

BROKEN HALLELUJAHS

❖ ❖ ❖

POEMS BY

SEAN THOMAS DOUGHERTY

AMERICAN POETS CONTINUUM SERIES, No. 104

BOA EDITIONS, LTD. ❖ ROCHESTER, NY ❖ 2007

First Edition
07 08 09 10 7 6 5 4 3 2 1

Publications by BOA Editions, Ltd.—a not-for-profit corporation under section 501 (c)
(3) of the United States Internal Revenue Code—are made possible with the assistance
of grants from the Literature Program of the New York State Council on the Arts; the
Literature Program of the National Endowment for the Arts; the County of Monroe, NY;
the Lannan Foundation for support of the Lannan Translations Selection Series; the Sonia
Raiziss Giop Charitable Foundation; the Mary S. Mulligan Charitable Trust; the Rochester
Area Community Foundation; the Arts & Cultural Council for Greater Rochester; the
Steeple-Jack Fund; the Elizabeth F. Cheney Foundation; the Chesonis Family Foundation;
the Ames-Amzalak Memorial Trust in memory of Henry Ames, Semon Amzalak and Dan
Amzalak; and contributions from many individuals nationwide.

Cover Art and Design: Steve Smock
Interior Design and Composition: Richard Foerster
Manufacturing: BookMobile
BOA Logo: Mirko

Library of Congress Cataloging-in-Publication Data

Dougherty, Sean Thomas.
  Broken hallelujahs / Sean Thomas Dougherty. — 1st American pbk. ed.
    p. cm. — (American poets continuum series, no. 104)
  Includes bibliographical references.
  ISBN 978-1-929918-92-8 (pbk. : alk. paper)
1. Experimental poetry. I. Title.

PS3554.O8213B76 2007
811'.6-dc22
                                2006029931

BOA Editions, Ltd.
Nora A. Jones, Executive Director/Publisher
Thom Ward, Editor/Production
Peter Conners, Editor/Marketing
Glenn William, BOA Board Chair
A. Poulin, Jr., President & Founder (1938–1996)
260 East Avenue, Rochester, NY 14604
www.boaeditions.org

NATIONAL
ENDOWMENT
FOR THE ARTS

State of the Arts

NYSCA

Contents

IV

Our relationship to the dead continues to change, because we continue to love them.
—Anne Michaels

For my family and our Poppa, Joseph Kriesler (1919–2002)

 I

The Sentence

Between the sweetness at the end of our hum the sentence says come
in through the skin's transparent address. The sentence: a motionless
river. The sentence: a needle through your umbilical cord. But to hold
a bow: to be still, the sentence as violin, before the first note defines the
air, gives birth to the borders of silence, like a pinwheel whose edges
spin with wind. *Sexual definition*. No entrance but into the unseen. The
sentence as piñata. The childhood drama—to strike blind and then the
candy, tiny wooden animals, gold-foiled coins, falling through the lift-
ing, the effort, and the children groping with glee. This "public text,"
memory—against the humiliation of not being picked. Out of all atrocity
can we find the hurt child? Out of all great empathy—the hand reach-
ing into the ditch. To burst open the seams, to spin *in*. A sentence whose
seeking is in. You cannot erase the child, the sentence says. The sentence
that says *child* says it, for your eyes speak for your hands. To make. This
ends, open. *Against homeland, let there be odes to the useless like light trembling
regiments to lay down their arms, let there be rivers, Cyclops, interruptions into the
story I wish to tell—to not tell—to elide, excusez moi, there is pollen drifting off the
flowers in the old woman's stand by the train station, a boy in a brilliant green shirt
is painting his face with white paint, in the empty music case he will use to catch
coins is the ghost of his sister's viola, and as he moves, speechless, the whiteness of
his face tells us of her long dying, his hands press against nothing making shapes.*
A sentence named Goya. For the sentence wishes to press against only
the whiteness of the page, to give form, sulfuric, as memory suddenly
could go it was I am you are it seems do I what's that your aviary inside
the house of the earth your face the name for these topaz seeds, gold
wheat called prayer. A sentence named Peruvian mines. A sentence as
dark as American money—let drown in its own unraveling, entwined
as intestines, antiseptic. A sentence that does not tell a family drama,
rain-blurred, wind-washed, precision—resists becoming the census for an
opera. The sentence as census for the opera. A clown-laughed sentence.
In the ballroom of the backyard, your laughter, in the steam of your
breath: we eat paella, the dish of the sea our tongues tell, each muscle we
waltz in scholarly diction transformed into accordion keys. After dinner
we gather thistles, we eulogize your right shoe left out on the lawn, the

sentence: upside down glamorous not-obvious, asymmetrical overlooked joy so long sought. The sentence is a chanteuse, unretired, stirring with a strong sigh, a suffering sparrow, outside a gray downtown Nativity scene, this last sentence: a small, winged thing rising—

Your Voice After Desnos

Your voice is the evening's calligraphy of starlings. Your voice is a surgeon's stethoscope. Your voice is the last bar open after Desnos. Your shiny voice. Your voice of broken graffiti. Of pawnshop tickets. Of musical instrument grass. Your voice of locked puppets. Your rib-caged voice. Full of strings. Blue, fragile bees.

The Long Waiting

In the small room inside my mother's chest, a weeping sound that whispers across the tall grass of late summer carries my mother toward her childhood, my running mother running through the sand in summer rain toward her father's lifting hands. My mother is a laughing sound at five, —mother she calls to my grandmother, a hunger made of kisses. When the cancer ate his hunger, my Poppa, leaning on his bed, told my mother *I can no longer taste the bread.* Social worker, scholar, he pamphleted for Socialism—the ideology of the century just ended, my mother frightened by the frailness of her father's hand—we are birthed into the sterile light, the social weight we enter with the cutting of the cord. Across our bellies, the tied knot our true tribe. Socialism's promise: the sound of any child sharing bread. Yiddish was a second language for Hungarian Jews. The rain against my grandfather's windows. Summer rain: the sound of memory's shoes. At the Social Welfare office, paperwork piled on Poppa's desk, the names of the hungry my grandfather worked to help. The hungry men, women, children at the shelter called him Joe. Hungry, my mother left my grandfather in that room, a socialism of rain falling, four walls of waiting. She sat with the hunger of grief, picked at a plate of sardines, onion, bread. Hungary was a cracked jewel when my great-grandmother boarded the boat at twenty—in 1912, arrived hungry at Ellis Island: The copper torch burned the night, Hungary became a left place, a last leaving. Alone across the cold Atlantic, she carted a trunk of books. *Across* means to depart, or to arrive? My mother reaches for her father's hand, *Hungry* she asks him, bones, barely breathing, *Water* he asks, closes his eyes. My mother feels the water closing above her head. My great-grandmother's water broke in 1919. Five years later, thin and hungry from fever, she died. My grandfather sips his water slowly, *I haven't thought about her in a long time.* Water in his eyes, my mother puts a cloth upon his chest. The social agency sent nurses that night. On the *George Washington*, water was passed in a bucket. Waterfalls of voices that rode into the harbor. Mother, do you ever wonder on this woman, the grandmother you never kissed? Long after her death, the husband who disowned his son, water of my grandmother's Christian birth? Across the aisle my grandfather's side was empty. Across the Atlantic his rebel

14

mother knitted, not prayed. Across is to arrive, or to depart? Someone has entered the room. *Water* my grandfather whispers, his black eyebrows knitted. Across the deck my great-grandmother hummed, spray washing across the boots of Czechs, Slavs; the moon spoke Hungarian, bathed her black hair with silver light. Across her chest an old Magyar touched the sign of the cross. My great-grandmother reached for a chair—parochialism of the rural poor, the pogroms, Socialism promised a world of *workers sharing bread.* Regina Moskowitz crossed with a thousand other seamstress revolutionaries. Mother who died when my grandfather was five. O Mother, what is this ghost womb calling from the sky? Mother, I hear you in the kitchen sobbing. My grandfather is dead: Across the ocean, is he traveling? He is just a child. The summer rain, is it carrying him toward his mother? Is she calling him to Hungary? Is she singing lullabies in Yiddish? *Can you hear?* Her eyes are weeping prisms.

Canzone Sprayed with Graffiti

To spin, pilate, Bolshoi leap, the limbs thin, choreographing
The wind, or the light falling like Vermeer, a portrait
The canvas squints, these boys in baseball caps with their radio
Transforming the block into yellow, green, red, breaking
The syntax of the sidewalk, re-inventing verbs
They pivot on one hand and become a new form——
A new thing sung through the bones, a new law of motion
The body didn't know it could bend, a subway sonata,
A yellow taxi in A minor, an operatic move to the hoop
Chanted tenor, they are the shadows' rest when it rains,
For what is the wind's thrush through the leaves, pigeons
Cooing for black bread scattered by Babushka's hands?

Love: the comings and departures, the station's stand.
That gather into a waltz, hear the lions call across the boulevards.
This rebellion. This broken shine. Limp-lettered. Longitude
Of limbs. This rising. Asphalt forgotten. Sparrows. For bread loves
Goya's black paint. Basquiat's slashed face.
For what is moonlight on a battlefield. Love: let there be
Open hydrants splashing summer day foot-shine. The el shuddering
Graffiti across the skyline. The unwritten opera of the Brooklyn Bridge.
A Chinatown stall, eggplant, veined cabbage, the chalked letters
On the wooden boxes, written carefully with a concerned hand.
Against silences these signs. A woman brushing her daughter's black hair
In a Bronx park, the saxophone player closing his eyes, hear the coins

Drop like Eucharist into his brown open-mouthed case.
These strangers leaning like trees into each other's shoulders.
Hear the Michelangelo of their muscles flex.
Newspapers like leaves rustle by the taxi stand.
Choreography for a marionette opera: waiting on the sidewalk
For the light to change, pedestrians humming the chorus line
Of bread crumbs in the wind. Verdi in the bus driver's hands.
The lithography of leaflets plastered on the subway wall.

A girl humming Beethoven's Ninth by the library's lions.
Chalk-lines of a body fallen from a fire escape,
All the writings we read or let dissolve into illegible noise,

Like Rauschenberg. The wind spells the way to read, listen:
To the children calling rhymes like wind chimes from every stoop.
On the east side the Ukrainian girl listens to the wind, she writes
The wolves are howling on the steppes. The pines are snowed
With sorrow her sister sighs. Such love is gift and grace.
The Rabbi leans into the script, a voice is gathered made of lines, curves.
Alvin Ailey taught the wind ballet, he studied how a leaf leaps.
Pavlova memorized how a leaf falls. The body shifting into
Sleep. This sense of shape, this sound. This blessed noise:
Illegible as Pollack the canvas quakes us to the core, to stutter
At the drip of paint. Who turns away turns away from drowning—

Why celebrate the muted halls? The blue child plays the violin.
What's written in the tape the runner snaps? The ball that banks
Off glass, limbs long as letters reach? Shreds of newsprint pasted
Into speech. Not to watch the rerun replay rehashed trash.
The adolescent be-bop pre-bop re-bop: bored?
But as the director cuts, a certain light evades the critic's eye.
Though trite, a joyful corporate glint in bodies gleams
For two teenagers who sway slow on a playground swing,
Could there be love despite the clichéd map? The earnest trap?
The hum of hands, the chain-linked seat. Their dangling legs
A dance. And what of the choreography of glances on the street?
For the body's broken jazz. A crowd of strangers clapping,

A boy bends his body to the beat, pops his joints
Into graffiti: Giotto reaching for an angel's halo.

Dear Pistachio

My dear impertinent pistachio,
my lady-slipper's largesse,

my eucalyptus, my Calypso bent calla lily,
my earth-cauled cauliflower,

O my babushka'd cabbage,
my dear ragamuffin ragweed—

my heliotropical sunflower,
my honeyed locust,

my vituperative violet, my delicately cloaked
artichoke—my lima bean,

Lie down my shady lady-fern, my blue
bell, my

willow, my rapturous
rain-washed

radish.

II

The Dark Soul of the Accordion

~

My grandfather does not sleep among the roots. His ashes are in an urn. His ashes are hidden in my grandmother's downturned eyes. My grandmother sits and stares out at the garden in my aunt Nora's house. She is waiting for the crocuses to bloom. She is waiting for the tulips to open the palms of their petals to cup the milky light. What does it mean to die in winter?

My grandfather died in late summer and all winter was our own death. We walked among the scattered children shouting as they pulled their plastic sleds carving up the hillsides at Frontier Park. Red-mitten blossoms in the snow, hats pulled low down to eyes, able to sit at Avanti's over a dark cup of coffee, flip through a book of Spanish poems, arguing with the translation's inept understanding of the vagaries of Lorca's syntax. To die in winter is to translate the cold sorrow of the heart into the slumber of the grass, to hear its one note quiet breathing beneath the snow. To know the sailboats moored as hulls to part the water toward the line where sky becomes the world. Sailboats: palmed hands of wind. To heal in winter requires forgetting, the way the snow turns the landscape into sleep. For in winter the world forgets its grieving. For in winter, the world becomes a silence made of snow. A silence made of breathing, the crunch of ice and salt beneath your boots. In the falling sky, we are able to refind our womb-shape, our shape of solitude against the noise and detritus of grieving. In that silence we are able to unlisten and so begin to live again in the simple ways that living calls, to get up each day, to break the eggs at breakfast. Boil a pot of black coffee and not begin to weep for the sudden recollection of his hand, the black hairs brushing your face, and the strong coffee breath of his kiss as he lifted you as a child in the morning. Once again you are able to tie our shoes.

~

The rain outside increased and my grandfather fell into a morphine induced sleep. We could hear him wheeze upstairs in his room. I sat downstairs on the couch with my father randomly clicking the television with the sound off, getting up to stare out at the streetlight, the sounds of traffic from Congress, cars in the rain, destinations under their treads. I stood in the doorway half a dozen times smoking a cigarette, watching the smoke spiral up into the rain. More than once my grandfather woke and was calling to a name I couldn't understand.

The snow of my grandfather's eyebrows, the passing streets, endlessly fenced yards and children who run in their own wilderness. My grandfather's hands are the edge of somewhere weighted by its own rage, a voice shadowed with the blue of saying goodbye. Abandoned lots. Where there is the weight of hunger, my grandfather is there. My grandfather's reaching hand is an answer to all the bitterness, to the tongue's eating, and the stone's fatal flaw. Where there is the dismissive, he is the stutter in their speech. My grandfather's hands are a dark dusting, the raw faces, the stumped.

For which rules are cages, my grandfather crosses out. Walking down Congress Street the men call his name. His face opens a city block, his face is a braid against the hours spent searching for loose change. His face is a cup of coffee and a place to smoke. A place to smoke is not much to ask from the world for a man's life. My grandfather worked his life to create rooms of light and smoke and bread. To lean into them against the splintered wind.

~

In the summer the runaway children gather on the streets of Portland, Maine. Their torn jeans, their blue hair, their tattoos.

~

The day my grandfather died.
Birds. When I cup my hands over my face and try to remember that day I see birds in the blue distance. I am standing in the kitchen holding the receiver and my father is telling me I need to return. I am angry with my father because I was just back visiting with my wife and son and the visit went bad. Everyone was so grief-stricken and sad that no one knew how to talk to one another. We had wanted to stay with my grandfather but ended up leaving sooner because we thought there wasn't room at their house. So typical of my family, of my own life, this inability to say what we need, what we want. Even at such an important time.

And then my grandmother called and I heard in her voice birds. Such a faraway sight, they were rising into the sky over the lake. And it was as if I could see myself outside myself. I was standing there in the kitchen holding the receiver of the phone but in my mind I was already returning, already returning to where I was from, like birds flying over the Great Lake, headed toward the nesting grounds. I hung up and called the airline. The next day I was sitting in a small silver jet rising up over the Great Lake.

~

My grandfather's eyes are rain across countless countries. My grandfather's eyes are closed.

~

Leaning back into my seat, closing my eyes—what I remember most about that flight, no one sat next to me.

~

The nighttime is an endless August of sirens and rain. I am walking past the closed shops of Congress Street, the used book stores and dive bars. I am walking past the brewery and the shipyard, past the boutiques and the bathing suit models, the mannequins in their perfect gestures. I am walking past the yellow blur of taxis, and the last drunks, stumbling home. I am walking because my grandfather is dying and I cannot sleep. The insomnia of the grieving. The insomnia of third-shift workers laid off, now home watching TV. The insomnia of women walking to sell their bodies along the bay. The insomnia of old women whose husbands are dying, can you hear them as they rise to walk into the bathroom and run the water of the sink, hear them fill the glass and drink slowly, hear them flick off the light? Can you hear them fold their bodies like paper cranes beside the dying, listening to their husbands' hearts? Can you hear them lying with their eyes awake through the night? Can you hear the insomnia of daughters who talk in their sleep? Or this—the insomnia of the rain, how it loses its lullaby, how it calls the teenage girls outside to climb over the cemetery steps and sit smoking cigarettes on the tombs of the long dead. The insomnia of car tires in the distance. The insomnia of the rough betrayals. Of late night Laundromats. The shabby insomnia of hospital waiting rooms, of restaurant windows, smoky with human breathing, the insomnia of cars at stop lights, of bad girls and incantations. The insomnia of the doll's open eyes, out in the alleyway's trash. Of working and recollections. The insomnia of afternoons before the rain began. Before pawn shops and Edith Piaf. Before the haunting metro of

Hart Crane and Lorca's last laugh. Before a cigar store in Amsterdam and here in America the music of fears. Before his mother brought milk. And he couldn't move. Before the Angel who wrestled with Jacob, and the mountain, brilliant and frowning. The insomnia of the mountain. Before temples and photographs of W. C. Fields. Before Fritos. Before baseball cards. Before stumbling drunk without teeth. The insomnia of waking no one. The insomnia of awaiting the dead.

~

Golem, come to me tonight and save my grandfather. Lift him with your clay hands.

Golem, how far have you traveled? Golem, you do not answer. Golem, you stand by the side of the bed. Your massive head, your Dutch-boy haircut. Golem you have come but you can do nothing against Death. Death rides the razored rain. Golem, you are clay.

~

I have come for you my child.

See me, my dark hair my eyes. Feel my hands across your rough cheeks. I will lift you like water. Into the cradle of my two arms. We will rock across the great ocean. We will fly through the palace steeples. Across the mountains and the rivers, the chaotic streets, the wars. See me, my dark hair my eyes. Hear my lullabies, let them lift you from the bed. Help me tie the sheets into a sail. We will fill it with our breathing. See it billow. We are sailing on the wind of our leaving. See me, my dark hair my eyes. Why do you cry? There is no more weeping. Let the ashes of our bodies become the Braille the wind spills. Let it spell the shapes of song. Touch the earth. It is a last leaving. Touch my hand. Find your name in my palm. Place your arms around my neck. You are my first child, my precious grieving. See me, my dark hair my eyes. We are never leaving. Into the cradle of my two arms you are climbing. Through the window we are flying. Over the great sea, the wars, the palaces. The children are all finally sleeping. The rain is carrying us over the streets the forgotten streets, I am bandaging your bruised shin, where I wiped your chin, where I nursed. Open your eyes and see me. My dark hair my eyes. My fever has broken. I am here. My child, I am calling. I was never gone.

~

Wires and tubes. His body thin as wind. His collar a cave. It was hard to see my grandfather like that. It was hard to see him struggling to shape sounds, to make words work. It was hard to hear. The morphine stuttered. The pain eased, then gripped. He closed his eyes. The past tense. The present tense.

"Poppa?"
"I don't want to leave... I will miss everyone. She was smart, you know."
I went to touch his arm.
"Who, Poppa?"
"My mother." He turned and looked at me
"Rose, you mean—?"
"She traveled here alone... I don't know. I can't blame them. They were peasants. What did they know? They didn't know anything. The village followed them. They brought the ways of not trying. There were no books in the house, you know, only prayer books—"
"Wouldn't your mother read to you?"
He mumbled something I couldn't understand. His head nodding, his eyes closing again. I couldn't help staring at the tubes, the oxygen tank beside him like a nightmare. I couldn't help wanting to hold him and yet he looked so fragile, thin as paper. Thin as wind.

~

Hours pass and I can't remember my mother not crying.

~

Poppa, why do they come to you at night?

They come to bring me black bread and holy wine.

What do you hear when you close your eyes?

I hear her at the window singing Yiddish lullabies.

Why is the light of the dead yellow as a sunflower's face?

It is the fields of the dead we walk through on the way to our childhoods. Each flower sways with the love of someone we are leaving.

What does the rain spell for you?

It spells the lost name of my mother's mother. It spells Why did you desert us?

Whose voice is the rain, Poppa?

It is my voice. It is the voices which carry me away from you. If you listen you can hear your voice. A chorus. The temple is full of sparrows, it is saying. It is the voice of every human, which is to say, it is the voice of every Jew.

Who is the woman pushing the cartload of bread?

She has no name, only an echo.

Is she coming to feed us?

She is awaiting all of our dead.

~

Can you hear the accordion? Its golden keys. The opening wheeze of its bellows, and then the orchestra of its breath. There were accordions on the Death trains, that sewed the rain into a shawl to cover the dead. Smashed accordions littered the barbed-wire ditches upon arrival. What were those last songs? Those last sorrow songs the people of Uzhgorod sang? Did they already whisper Kaddish for the dead? Accordion of the dead children. Accordion of the Gypsy and the gavel. Say can you hear the accordion this night on 6th Street? Someone is stopped at a red light with their windows down, and a song in Spanish, perhaps Colombian, is filling the night with cabaret. An accordion is a kind of lungs that speaks the language of the dispossessed, the dead. This is why it is the instrument of Argentina, with its duende and atrocity. And in the Polish Polka there rises a joy against the slaughterhouse, the steel mill, the coal mine. With each step the room shudders and shifts. Once in a bar in Buffalo, New York, I witnessed the accordion player lean into the keys, high on his stool, the brushes shimmering the drum tops into rain across Ellis Island. We were all drunk and forgetting.

And here in the hollow hall at Ellis Island I hear the accordion begin to play and the Magyars spinning in their Bohemian dresses. See the beautiful girl posed on the wall in black and white, the billowing folds of hand-woven intricate thread. The accordion my grandfather heard when he was a child and rode the hay cart through Uzhgorod. The accordions they played on the *George Washington* as it departed from a German port in 1912 on the edge of war, and Regina Moscowitz leaned on the rail to watch the Lutheran steeples and the dockworkers fade into the fog. Was there anyone there for her to wave goodbye to? What did she carry in her hands? Perhaps she wore a new hat she had just bought in a little shop in Budapest, a dozen blocks from the Imperial Palace. She kept it in its box all the way to Germany, carried it like a child, rested it like a lapdog on top of her black trunk. On the boat, in the fog of late summer, she closed her eyes and dreamed of pigeons eating bread from her outstretched hands.

~

My great-grandmother's signature on the Ellis Island Web site: It's curvatures, swirls, its wrist whip and press. It's hand weight. This signing that signifies the arrival of a part of who I am here on this earth. I am the first one in my family to witness these words, this name. No one else has seen it. For a long time I sit staring at the screen, and then I begin to cry. The remembrance of my grandfather dying, and the unbearable weight of him as a child watching a room full of strangers weeping for the death of his mother. And it is this weeping that I realize calls me to find out about Regina. How I watched my own mother wail uncontrollably, her body shuddering with grief for the death of her father. And in this, there is no solace, no consoling story for this grief. But there is a calling, and the calling is this name, spoken by my grandfather as he merged halfway between this world and the next, or nothing.

For the wind is whipping the rain tonight. And I get up and walk to the room of my son, the light from the hallway falling across his sleeping eyes.

~

When a Jew dies he must die whole. Wrapped in a white cloth. The family drops a handful of dirt to signify the finality of death. If there is a coffin, it is a plain one made of wood, so that the body can return to the earth.

My grandfather asked for his body to be cremated. He asked for no service. This was as far from a Jewish burial as could be requested. Only afterwards did I think of this, of his final refusal, his final turn from his childhood identity.

Once, a good year before he died, for a reason I cannot remember, I asked him, "Do you ever still consider yourself a Jew?" He didn't hesitate. "What is a Jew? If a Jew is someone who follows the Torah, no? But is that what makes a Jew? And if so, what good for others? What walls?"

~

Clocks and maps change to the falling rain. In the absence between things. The space between branches, as much the branches as the wood itself. One must listen. The armies rise and fall, the broken waves. The children crying on the starboard port. Bombs dive from planes, trains' slow departure, the last callings. Can you hear? Can you see the rails now overgrown, see the yellow pages of the bureaucrats handwriting? What lotus blossom wilts? What temple do we find overgrown with vines and weeds? The statues falter, the rain-worn eyes of emperors. Look for me in the absence between things.

~

Evening came and he heard his mother calling. It is this intangibility of answers, a kind of awareness of presence that was evoked by my grandfather's dying speech that I cannot let go—a collage of fragments, almost-felt perceptions, continuously unraveling threads that shimmer like rain. A novel of not-arrivings. An autobiography of *absence*. For without *absence* there is no is. This is *not* recollection. But transformation. A collaged history. The horizontal spatiality of memory that does not actually exist. The imagination's many mirrors: A brown button. A ripped ticket. A signature. A mass grave. An accordion. A lullaby. An ocean liner. A witness.

~

The waiting, and the longing, the leaving and the night's embrace. The last embers that rise from the fires, and the gathering at day's end. The women walking heads down from the textile shops, their heads wrapped in sweat and babushkas, their husbands' beards clean and swaying as they talk with their hands. The nodding and the translating, the bread and the bartered fish, the books in my small hands, my belly growing.

III

Oberek

Let us droop
      Into weeping
Sky, dance
      & kneel
The trees' luck.
      My eyes blue,
I eat home.
      You sleep sigh.
To bop breath.
      To bleed brass,
An ache born
      With rain blind:
Your voice:
      Begged fruit
Blushed
      Grace grows
My want, lugs
      My lit world:
The deep dusk
      Of praise——
Come sun
      Sing
A saint rusted
      Latch, a hurt
Church, a dog
      Howled
A-way-road: widowed
      Smoke, spiraling
Ash, ember
      Rebuke
The jukebox's
      Tender
Tongue.
      Come home

My bread
      Risen cathedral quiet:
Let our feet
      Lift the earth—
Let us step
      With wind
Warbled spin.

Pas de Deux

Do you Merengue to the marimba, Salsa to the zither,
Waltz to the wah wah co? Maybe you two

Tango the two step to the Mississippi Watusi? Mash the Potato,
holding onto the ladle as you belly up Break Out

in Electric Boogaloo? Or do you put on your red shoes
and Shock the Monkey, wear the carpet thin Running the Man

in perfect Funky Chicken? Do you Shinto on the roof
of a Pinto? Look spooky as you bless the Kabuki?

Or do you both swivel your hips, side by side Boot Scootin
Boogie, or Tush Push a Cajun Jive, a Cadger's Caper,

a Jockey's Jig Yale, Ma Navu listening to *I'm going
back to Cali*, Karim the Sota or polish up on your Pappa Joe

over kielbasa and kimchee? Maybe you go Skinny Dipping
with the Chelmsford Assembly while sipping martinis,

a last Night Cap through a Fan? Unhook the clasp pins
on Ms. Pike's Cockle Shells. O Row Well Ye Mariners

for the Sham Hareh Golem is Tango Poquito—do you Lindy Hop
Limbo to Rag Time? Or dress drag to Texas Cha-cha

all the way up to Contra? O Grinding the Green Corn,
O shimmery scaled Dragon Fan. Do you Stroll

in cerulean blue Cumbia and Mazurka the Morcamba
Bay Zenska Siptarska Igra Krozek Farmer's Quadrille?

Do you grind your Fandango? Do you Freak the Flamenco
on down to the Butterfly ground? Bumping Kinka

or Kpanlango? Takeda equal rights for Kenya, Zulu apartheid
to the beats of the Pharcyde? When one is caught in a Twist,

blame it on the Bossa Nova, my brother. For tonight
is Louisiana Saturday Night and the beer is iced Polka

with Cotton-Eyed Joe twirling Tambourine Une Piassi Ici.
Do you let go your Scalps? Do you take turns leading?

Oberek: Warsaw in Spring

A false cloud—

A metallic wing,
Like a fist

Across your grandmother's
Upturned eyes,

A-for-instance
That swept

The walls:
Vacancy

Of what isn't, once
Was—not the kind

Of thing someone
Long ago

Hoped, humming
Among the shops

Of bread, the brick
& brac, speaking:

The grass
Begins to bend,

Like lovers
In a war

Ravaged country,
On the eve of peace:

Who turn in the park
Reinventing

The dusk—

Brief Blues

Where you gone? Drowned
In dogwood blossoms? Like lilies
From dead archangels' wings
Littering the lawns, the magnolia's

First petals fallen. Where have you gone?
I flip through the yellow pages
To find a section on grieving,
Spit-shined & honeycombed.

Where have you gone? Dutch
Elm disease, the boulevard
Barren, the nude shadows
Of bare limbs, amputees, asbestos

In the walls. Mockingbirds
& half drunks. The blues
Piano man, a hornet's nest
Like makeshift 3:00 A.M. sorrow.

Where have you gone? O what
Childhood's not recalled, the Queensboro's
Arpeggios, scalpels, & scales—
Your grandmother's cotton mouths

& crocuses, red dirt letters,
The calligraphy of dust—swan
Drifted woman, Lafayette-born
Sleepwalker. Where have you taken

My hands? In this city
Of psychotherapy & skyscraper'd
Acetylene torches, a hundred stories
High, petrified in black & white

Photos—what 4/4 time?
On a beaten bus, a train load
Of coal, a burning, a thrush.
Where shopping, in the bagger's slow

Hands, a kind of insistent someone
Damaged. This song. This brief
Blues asking—

The Sky Inside

My grandfather's hand opens and there is a sky inside. The sky is blue above the hayfields of Western Hungary. It is the Uzhgorod sky. Inside the field of my grandfather's palm is a tiny hay cart, pulled by a slow-paced mare, with white-tipped tail, a woman with a red babushka gathering (some indigenous flower) on a far hillside. A (bird) flies over my grandfather's wind-tossed hair——he is laughing at a joke in a language I do not understand, a tiny laughter like the wheeze of a sick child, there in his breathing, what is that roughness——then the sandpaper against my ears, the cough that pulls back the walls to this room. *This room.* The open curtains and the day gray with the threat of rain. My grandfather's nostrils hooked up to the oxygen tank. He opens his mouth to breathe like a carp, gasping. I want to close my eyes but I reach for his arm. His hand flexes slightly, closes, then opens again, like a lung. Like a tiny accordion. Adjusting the morphine. The anesthetic music.

After the War

Salsa disco jams late in the night what is left: summer softens the noise of the el and Mrs. Blanco calling in Cuban Spanish for her *popolito*—O sad-eyed men in tiny felt hats, the bitter sweet yawning of folded chairs on the sidewalks old women sweep the dust of late summer. One grandma cutting the neck of the chicken in the back alleyway, the soccer balls careening like pushcarts up the avenue. No one is always hungry, around the kitchen, there is stirring biscuits and black coffee, votive candles and candelabras, the Sacred Hearts, prayings, headless fish—hard blues running against each other O mercy there are Orishas, a brief symphony, at the corner store, the dangerous shine "of a yellow dress," the hint of rain closing second-floor windows, a tune sings of wonderment translating the secretly loved sapphires of never leaving home, for a cousin carrying his duffel from the train station, for unpacking the first time, this amnesty of as much as love as corn bread and grits and the memory of their faces slowly changing into the intimate idiom, didn't know that Blue's black honey, praise cotton candy every day leaning toward somebody singing without looking or feeling your name slowly as if sweet-grass and sarsaparilla, the luminous dawn of crossing vacant lots, a father into the country, the humdrum imaginations, learning to eat noodles, the swaying music of bodies, bar men, sleeping of skirt swirlings, my mother coming home from the New York City welfare office, this slow dance might slip the beauty and the little shaky agency of loin aches between us hard like a sawed-off shotgun, Mr. Palmero's boy, ain't we beautiful, prisoners with space to breathe, morning gospel of growing toward—this last fruit of summer, "yearning for legitimacy" "origins of composition" or the sky, conceived mandolin brilliant rhythms of a strange afternoon—on the third floor after the war was over, a salt light, a sound as it was before, from the kitchen she is turning to catch his breath, from behind in the damp wind as you run carrying your duffel through the falling leaves they barely graze you.

All You Ask for Is Longing

Y not that year empty with strangers. Y not the silence of wanting.
Y not when we laughed with rain with something, lounging high,
touching your bare shoulders, when I was born.

Y not your long hair that turns within. When the sirens begin. Y not a
kind of disruption, a kind of rupture by *arrangement*.

Y not the archeology of Other. Y not limbs, tattoos, the DTs at dawn,
H's widow's hungering, sweating on the fire escape smoking in her
bra.

Y not out of style is loss. Your old clothes in boxes, someone's scrawled
name.

Y not from you as if dulled with liquor, on the bare mattress, your
open thighs. To step in their stillness was to become the word *erased*.

Y not a kind of rain, a kind of arms, a kind of shouting, after a while I
couldn't sleep without you.

Y not some of your friends when we were young, the one with stubble,
eyes like glass. When you were nothing.

Y not their frail bodies, shining.

Y not snow, the syllabics of suffering,
routine.

Y not elegies spray-painted on basketball courts, each stroke says
tomorrow I won't be here.

Y not waiting——thank you——ceaseless——passing of being human.

Y not my glance—stillness—blue listened for music in your room, an ascension overheard through the paper walls.

Y not the way we'd map the cracks in the ceiling—the dim bulb absence hummed.

Y not you, why can't I—you in this city at closing hour, this strange going improvised ravine, summer rain among the living.

Y not toward your story, green indecipherable shadows, faces I want would, longing, to cathedral—

Y not two voices that diminuendo, the point at which what is revealed, is what leaves—

Shift

Hit shift: SUPER FLY fro on the subway between Parliament and Post-Apartheid—*Properly*—remember near-chanting that down on the first syllable in the club rocking gin and bass—She does it *Properly*—long gone like Car Wash suds hipster Zoot Suits against chains—yet four millions sleep barred brethren you sleep in your *exploration of silence* Pulitzer hip for the noise is too loud but I say shout Bring on Da Noize Da Funk the P Funk Make my Funk pump in the back of yo trunk make the Soul Shimmy sway remake the world out of red clay beans and rice Jambalaya mish max mix it up Cajun with couscous on the side like a long playing LP solo like Fred Anderson of the Chicago Art Ensemble playing free form candlelight moonshine American wrinkles around his mirrored syntax layered History riffs wind wayward redolent White America the officer compounds of Christ's gated-community the camps of aesthetic fascists lost in their fragmentation ironic sardonic bitter tenure instead of trembling ecstatic in beats shaking Groove Things sunshine Blame It On The Boogie Woogie to Avenue B damn times Dizzy times Good Times two plus two is three in the 21st Century so astonishingly uttered these Loisada language dreams toward Nueva York Orange County rich white girl ska band gone solo Super Fly white female video uttered for each the word love for each is Memorial shoemaker shopkeeper in the New World for the Old World for the lost names and the Yahrzeit light for *the nobody who would know* for the Hebrew and the Holocaust for the Woolworth's counter and the young men who refused to leave for the mothers who faced nightsticks and knuckles and the ghosts embrace coral necklaces train yard my people goat-slaughtered who are my People—all people—is this possible—Father sleep late for the factory is closed the shift differential is spent in the neighborhood of lost nickels in the church services in the Barrio where the priest was born in the blessing of English-less-ness in the Godfather's grace in the lost tongues in the tongue spoken for gratitude is a bus ride home from work for running with our backs to the flames to fall in love easily and you aren't afraid the door is closed for wearing braces is a signifier of class for struggle for a cigarette after coffee for our mothers' varicose veins and the long walk up the third flight of stairs for a hard-boiled egg and a bottle of water in the hot sun leaning over the fields for the rum runners and the grape pickers spinning assimilated names in my hands I am a man something to lift to pick to shelf to make to play to pause to hold to sift to say my life is more than this signature this card passport license face to say I learned no I learn against this *aqui* to shimmy-shake hunger of the old dialect the new dialect where we slept interlaced in the fields of everything earned to earn incarnate confession of the kitchen broom sweeping the dust out of the Tombs where they took the secret scrolls hear the young babushka'd woman brush the crumbs off the counter at the last open diner where the Super Fly rest after a long night of something shaking with their spangles and their tight pants and their bodies' imagination before the next shift their own identity that shine that digging out that last cigarette after coffee and the slow jam and the new steps and the new hair and the new length for the skirt you just bought that new long-playing single that new language bearing down the track needed washing off your mascara taking off your uniform untying your hair the radio playing marimba of the red ribbon your man's hands his dirty hands from work and love and need a burning a burning river.

Black Earth

North American name-droppers with the latest fashion, elliptical,
apolitical, Harvard-inscribed Brooklyn literati
on the avenue of winter trees, they gleam. Haircuts class.
Let the dead worship Greek gods, continental theory. Give us
corn bread and grits with gravy. Hear the old Jewish shopkeeper
dusting anarchist manifestos on the Lower East Side, the otherwise
quite forgotten, hungry outside the Guggenheim, in Youngstown
the sound of a belt, your uncle returned from the army, dying
in the light that falls in funeral torches—baptism of desire
and the butcher and the rain-veiled vending machines, punk kids
begging for fare anywhere. Pitchforks and hospitals. Born
in the bread of the Allegheny. A boy spits chewing tobacco
off the trestle's high tracks. In the city of dead steel. A girl sharpens
a blade against the curb. As the dogs circle, what terror
in the presence of starving deer. On a night when the new moon
is not enough. Witnesses gather, faces lit like Byzantine saints.
We ear them. In the transient hotel, where the Russian novelist
types his first English letter, filling each page with black earth.

My Father's Fro in the Mode of Romare Bearden

Our shoulders touch to build a real peace within a heaven one

city   of my great-grandmother's sweet potato pie   magnolias

blossom   emerging   an embryo   the moon's shimmering

collective eye   tongues shudder   theory   okra a bed of witnesses

laid   so many Marvins sigh *Mercy Mercy Me*

conch shells   a sequence South Sides whenever we

sleep a sinuous cricket shines   my father's fro   a pregnancy

against draft cards everything   plain-spoken to awake   a new

alphabet   Georgia under lynchless skies Legba a cosmos of

delicate gourds Bootsy Collin's bassline   Sly playing in the

background of some backyard bash everyone shaking *something*

for dinner   the noose   a bullet   *They laughed as they hung Him*

from the trunk of the old sycamore Halos windless comes

Orishas   weeping in white robes my eyes turn in   the arms

of his hair   the silver grass   strung with stars   sea shells

Ellison invisible Dejembe   no "warring" I shall go *wearing*

Kente   Kent State   Ku Klux   sheets restitched into Egyptian sails Walt Frazier's sideburns   Monk choreographing the sound

that smoke shapes   A jukebox that plays nothing but versions of

Strange Fruit   Amadou Diallo's passport photo   at night how it

weeps   Molotov cocktails of monarch butterflies

Call Out

Rasa rasta, who took the funk, cut Walt Whitman's shaggy beard? Who donned Robert Lowell's glasses and forgot how to shake one's assets? Put the plunk in the piggy. Jiggie is junk slang. Dated and done. Dyed in white wool, the run. Who slavered over Marianne Moore's verses, while brother's filled hearses? Curses cut with hoodoo. Let the tombs tremor. Lace up those fat B-boy laces, though style be a changeable chum. Idioms are automatic. For the old man has donned his straw chapeau, and the ironclad steam engine is rolling through West Texas. What would Walt Whitman praise standing outside Attica, Folsom, the Paradise Penitentiary? For the Reggae's rum and the Cajun's hum hum, the accordion grieving slow bellows. Orange-plantation slaves: Haitian laborers unpaid. What salt shaft runs through Walt Whitman's beard, what shaggy shards? May the parchment petal. The fabric of a rhythm section. Literati Mafioso. Mariposa Spinoza. Bozos of the Brahman Brethren, grant-graced and tenured. All those long-playing LPs carted. Beardless, Walt Whitman rests his elbows on his thighs as the young men spin and fly. He is hidden on a subway car, on the ferry crossing to Staten Island. Brusque in Detroit, border crossing into Windsor. Stand down for the Homeland Police hate speech. VOX vocalized, shortwave letter. Kung fu Mau Maus in the magnolias. The last Yale graduate blows off the dusty tomes. Highlighting texts of disproportionate intellectual acclaim. Behold the paper butterfly and the iridescent puff as the old man stands up, wipes off his baggie pants. Word physicists sprawling coats of spray paint on underground passages. Let the record *scratch*—

Oberek for Etheridge Knight

In sky walls
Cats circle

Him stripped bare.
With red rims,

With kill skill
That dances

In doorways
Of glassed streets.

To whistle
His dope death:

Black Baptist,
Past mean bricks,

What weighted

That bare tree

That shimmered.
His shine sings.

His words womb

What sound sees.

The Day Biggie Smalls Died

(aka Christopher Wallace, March 7, 1997)

It was windless on Long Island Sound:
The weather that kills

from somebody else's life.
A note cut like Thelonious Monk

conjured, accidental beats,
shining texts certified diamond

disappeared—
Brooklyn grieved

five songs in his head
he never wrote down.

The DJ's discs spinning radiant
mythological badness.

A pair of stone prayers
attempting flight.

For hunger swung clean.
For hunger's one-track wail,

he stood. To know him
by his susurrations.

He blew seamless.
A city named breath.

The Black Frank White.
Becoming the traffic

to chance anything.
His dizzyingly adagio

delivery, a murmurous
dictionary, wreathed.

A torn riddle.

Somewhere on Planet Earth

In the dream of the perfect headspin, the cosmos
is backed by a funky ass bass line, the comets

are double-helixing into Stradivarius strings,
to separate pyramids from the posture

of a public playground, as the B-boys uprock
and suicide flip, the world revolves on its imperfect axis,

leap years flying into high five crowd swaying
slams, bent grasses bowing in ancient mathematics,

in the dream of the perfect headspin, the glass
of every broken window becomes the jagged

outline of Saint Teresa. The beat's tongue-driven
bravado, two turntables of Czar, professor

of the petroglyph, screenwriter
for the jackhammer's drill, resuscitation

after rainfall, in the Museum of Cole Porter
the skyline unveils the imperfect geometry

of the G clef, gangbangers brandishing
bouquets, never falling meteor of the human

body—day turning into night into day, the dark side
and the sun rising on the far moons of Jupiter,

unstringing the arpeggio of the Brooklyn Bridge,
a boy turns on his radio in a basement

somewhere north of Sarajevo, a tape mixed
in the citadel of East Cleveland, passed hand

to hand across continents of neon clubs
begins to bass, the perfect B-boy dreams

his fingertips push off the frozen earth,
the soles of his fat-laced sneakers rimmed

with quasars, cornfields, the 149th Street subway stop
in the Alhambra of the Bronx, like a turbine

he spins soundless as under sagging flotillas
of seaweed, somewhere in the South Pacific

the last great whales open their mouths to feed.

On the Heroic Ledge

Thelonious Monk's small hat, perched like a parrot
contrapunting the keys, his chords deep as if a garret

caught a note, held, broke, transformed into noise, transvestite
sounds: Major and minor at the same pound, ear-light

through the opaque trees like bourbon in a glass
tumbler, Monk did his little dance, hat in his hand, ask

a witness at the 5 Spot, hat like a crown, scattering
train tickets, palmfuls of sound, maps of meandering

rivers, humming his Pork Pie sigh
in Mississippi mud, Blues sued piano chimes,

moons of cigarette smoke rising against croon, the cavalry
stampedes the black keys, the ecclesiastical laboratory,

architect of the unexpected chord—a woman rejected,
a workday in hell, bus driver to Irony's Inn, elected

archprince of percussing the pedals, God's
righthand Sin, up there with Satchmo, pulling nods

like a chicken from a kettle, unpaid bills burned
on the landlord's ledge, outwit the hounds, churn

the butter brown, sound is reparation for 600 years
of Middle Passage bound, Harlem's rent in arrears

is rebellion, this black wedding, this cold rain churning
New Orleans's skeletons, workroom rhythms, alive

is more than living: corn bread, grits, collards
chain-gang driven stops, pail of slop, elevator

to the seventh level of Love, milk drowsy
breasts in a working man's hands, cobbling

worn-out shoes, lest one forget blistered
barbershop ear-language, basement furnace

banging, haloed bare, palms spread wide
he leaps (dues only God knows) to marry the air.

Embraceable You

Embrace me so we imagine the hint

of our unhurried bones, the idea

of the beautiful flickering

in all the ways we could get hurt—

betrayed by the purity of light,

almost tender, the way a pianist

leans into the blistering keys,

staggering with ruin, refusing to focus.

O my opulent marquee, my recipe

for shoes, bees, salt: stewed in a thimble.

Embrace me with candled crosses,

with the serious laughter

of symphonies, with the sadness

of harlequin hats. Embrace me

with the blowsy, minuet branches:

with the crumbling choreographies of chance—

In the Republic of Pantomime

To the bed,
           Blue shrine:

You come
           Bereft, a perfect

Prayer,
           Sacred shadow:

In the holy dark
           Breath, the shuddered

Shutter
           Of the heart's

Husk, let us suffer
           Like autumn, singed

Salt,
           Someone taken

In a glass room
           Shines—you: with open eyes

Hard—you: flower-shaped
           Seraph—you: whirlwind

Of leaf-lifted
           Light:

Naked

       A cappella

In the Republic

       Of Pantomime—

You climb

       Though the steep olive groves,

A woman

       Balancing buckets of well water—

Galicia

When you cut your hair,
the grass, broken-hearted,

whitened. The whimpering
of the rain. Each strand,

a missing—hermetic wide
mouth, rouged

honeysuckle soliloquy, iodine
dappled healing. Syllabic

& sanguine
shushedness, biographies

of back door broken hinges——
in the silent clippings, a woman

exhausted by the long walk
from the train, suitcase

of coal smoke
& Krakow. Moon pale

Magdalena, hair monosyllabic:
having cut off the raveling ends.

 **IV**

. . . love is a cold and it's a broken hallelujah . . .
——Leonard Cohen

Kowalski: A Historiography

A Polish paratrooper or pianist, grade-B movie director, Polka king—Kowalski the hip-hop artist crosses his arms on the peeling poster outside the Budapest Opera coffeehouse, bent-knuckled young intellectuals in metal-rimmed Kowalskish-gazing glasses scribble in furious Hungarian as I declaim Polish Hip Hop—O Kowalski Rhymes Krakow, crack or Post-Communist Angst? How do you emphasize *Ice cold* in Polish I ponder? The Danube's frozen waltzes, far from the Detroit River & Cobo Hall where the ghost of Killer Kowalski, the legendary wrestler grimaced—*Pimas Grimas* cry the posters for Kowalski the rapper whose syllables I mumble on the yellow subway, whole car graffiti like Bronx disciples splayed in bubble-lettered Hungarian. Graffiti scarred the crumbling facades of old stone SS headquarters. Peasant Kowalski fed the survivors outside the camps, trudged through the mud lifting the barely living. In Budapest our breath bloomed like Piotr Kowalski's silver spheres, 8 degrees by the Danube, we leaned into the razored wind my great-grandmother struggled through—Perhaps a Kowalski knelt before Our Lady of Czestohowa in the Polish church, a sanctuary from the sleet icing the cobblestoned streets, trams silvering electric lines, teenagers in headphones, westernized Budapest the most modern city in the world in 1900—my great-grandmother wrestled sunlight into her shawl, waited to catch a glimpse of Bartók, rain like sequins across her shoulders. In Yonkers years later she watched the reels of war, pomaded horseman marching to die in ditches. My grandfather would reach to eat the rain. My son scripts bubble letters across his notebook, blue graffiti like on these Israeli teenagers outside the Dony Cathedral. Graffiti is style without speech here—without translation the tags on stone remain unspoken, lines without noise. I touch the marker on the subway seat—politics or profanity? One of my students in Detroit explained, graffitiing the title to his story, about his father drinking Pabst, screaming at Killer Kowalski in Windsor, those joinings when his father held his hand, graffiti of his father's blue-veined fist turned tender. Archeologists found Hebrew graffiti on stones from fourth-century Pest, Jewish centurions buried defending the walled city. The ancient rabbis uttered the psalms. Budapest where the dead speak the syntax of Torah, a graffiti of what could have been—now a backdrop for spy flicks, cold-war nostalgia. In the black-and-white reels the children board the trains. *The last of us will soon be gone,* Suzanne utters outside Saint Stephen's cathedral. *It began with the graffiti, the arrow crosses—I've never seen any of the films they've made these years. Nothing made of celluloid can explain—it is like the weather. How can one really describe snow to someone in the desert?* These fictions we survive. She sips her coffee, *Survivor*—name for a mindless television game, a bad pop song, what meaning remains? She: one of the last witnesses, a reel that will soon unravel. We searched Budapest for some evidence of Kowalski's CD, flipped the stacks, the blank-faced clerks. Bernard Kowalski directed *Attack of the Killer Leeches*, a grade-B classic, or Lech Kowalski: punk underground director, DOA, son of Auschwitz survivors. These gritty Polish-American scripts. In Budapest my great-grandmother worked for the revolution, Budapest before the wars, the red pamphlets, the Zionists. Ady's black stone figure turned Budapest toward the 20th century. Ady's Budapest of erotic alleyways, opium cafés, and yellow trains. *Someone should make a movie of this.* My great-grandmother spooned pudding in the coffeehouse where we split a Dobos pastry, scribbled notes like rough graffiti sketches for whole car murals. We slept beside the hissing radiator, breath of Budapest graffitied my hands with steam—*Think: the rain was still the rain back then—Can you feel your great-grandmother running to the market beneath a black umbrella?*—this rain of funeral roses, Budapest city of roses, rain-dampened ripped poster of Kowalski you tried to peel from the subway wall. We never found Kowalski in the city of broken hallelujahs, Kowalski's Eastern European scratch. Budapest, where I unburied the murdered past. Rewound the reel of what could be—unvarnished the black paint to reveal the graffiti: *Regina Moskowitz forever running through the city of cobblestoned psalms.*

Fever Lullaby

Nights, those long-ago coughs, the winter of radiators hissing, I touched your fluttering lids, fever of forgetting nights we hung the ornaments on our limbs. Nights the stairwells lead to the rooms of ink-dark grievings, sieved with leaden light. The boy who ate paint on the stairwell, the lisp of his slow speech. Night, the apothecary's black bag. Nights the jury returns with the verdict of our childhood taunts, the playground's bruised knees. Effeminate child of the lonely leanings into the radio's held hands. Nights behind an alleyway of utterances, unsaid meanings, meaning *this is the harp I never held, those sentimental sorry's that could have saved us.* What syllable meant extraction, the pulled tooth. Under the pillow, a shining un-thing said.

These nights nobody claims. These nights of many. Or none. Collection plate of the Infinite. Observations like "or." Two dollar coins on the eyes of the dead. The women who still speak the mother tongue, keening. Nights of women keening into their fist-clutched shawls, orchid petals on the funeral parlor floor. Sweep away the nightshifts of knot-me-nots. Tongues twist to ask for prescriptions in the language not born into, in the language of practicing over the pages open in the grandchild's hand. Night, the immigrant: city of church spires, city of strangers sleeping on the subway platform, strangers headed toward another wage. Behind the lids, the village, blue paint and dust. Close the book and kiss the shoulder, love in any language means a country is our coupled limbs. What nation is this night, black threads in the old man's suit, hanging in the closet of questions. What's in the pocket of the man on the last bar stool. 3:00 A.M. is the noon of night, through the shadows of train stops, shuddering. Night-noon, the long sweep of flashlights. Foot shuffles to the cabinet, your mother's shaking fist. What night, long before I met you, your brother's knives. Glistening points, shivs. Parking lots I left stitches, touched my bruised eyes in the backseat of swerving taillights. Grant me this last question. NO-menclatures of the not-said. These long lists of not-sewing the fragments. Pieces collaged. Images torn to abstraction. Night, what renovations. What public housing inventory. The notches marked on the doorframe. Growing toward what child long gone, row where, squinting into the long hours against the numerologies of convictions, there in the stall behind the tomes—is it you—(the librarian pulls on her coat) not hearing the light's dark click.

In This Very Room

After arrested, baptism of everyone waiting in the parking lots of the fallen, urn earned. The white boy with the speech impediment, *Saint* in indigo ink on his mother's right arm. The green painted nails of her feet in flip-flops, her body leaning in a porch chair. She watches the smoke of her cigarette, watches the way sunlight falls on her hand, reaches up into the air in front of her face. She looks at the glint of her green nail polish. Pulls her hand down and begins to paint her middle finger—holding it up as if to say *fuck*—stroking it carefully with the tiny brush. Austere we are each man and woman. Stumbling dumb ragged beauty rescued, whorl sharked blue-veined bitter iris ungunned. Windless from what we most desire. *Sang* sounds Southern. Say it, *he sang a long wail for her absence.* We take the whang of it, carrying a bucket of peaches back from the farm. A little crazy with human loss, this stark grieven garment, coal-scaled, glittering fray at the corner of sleepwalk and voiceless, these blind refugees from the saffron fields, a misplaced shroud, gesturing sunflower, this lassoing of whatever is erased—to love them musically, bird-blissed, jeweled kisses, the country where bread is draped in green-desire, rummage sales of spider webs, hidden minor thirds, used rhinestones, rent we never learned meant—

Hades

Our separate worlds
Too small to eat,
Of family disputes

Swallow us.

~

When like kids
We carve a "fuck"
Into a climbed oak,

Dangling our bare toes
Like the just hanged.

~

My virtuoso,
Shall we recite the street's motto

To say *don't*
Nobody dare.

~

On the dead road
Are we not flames, vein-colored
Blue ghosts passing by

The way willows
Sigh,

The way swallows swoop
In endless loops?

Oberek

Empty hoops
Of white noise

And the clock
Of the text

Is a waltz
Of bird shoes

With wings red
To still light

Why stars veil
A kiln room

Perhaps fast
Will be born

With you last
Unwinding

The beautiful
Hierarchies

We turn limbs
To praise

Come sprung
Breath-filled sails

We writing
Are verbs

Against anthems
Against billboards

Against *disbelief*

We torn clouds

Swerve against
Bright shop windows

We a market
Two heads of cabbage

Balanced
Frightful & foolish

Fish stalls

Babushkas

Cobblestoned
Psalms

Vowel lisped

Accordions'
Abandonments.

Narrative I Don't Know How to Spell

Before you, everything drowned. Spoonful by spoonful, the river itself, even the mountain.

Far in the losing of things, on a Greyhound bus, long before music, long before exhausted our mouths cried out.

Before you, I lived without a *there.*

Obstinately forward, awaiting what——

My grandmother asleep on the couch with the clicker?

The nouns she says she forgets—to find such gentle recall, to shape the world into words.

Was it as simple as that, to plant a pronoun inside the chest, to announce this you to follow, forth and back.

Like music. Bowstrings plucked inside us. When our mouths conduct murmurous sounds, sighs.

And so it begins: with nothing more than the language of the grass on a hillside.

A sadness like a violin, a progression of chords toward the last question that begins and ends, elongates, like a vowel, shortens and suspends:

Nothing more than to know who I was in your hands.

What We Keep

Gray-blue rain far from your fingers tap tapping the letters of your name. In the blue hills above the graveyard we found at the edge of the woods, the fireflies we chased through the trees, drinking rum—were we singing or laughing when we fell soaked into the shadows of the grass? The chair in the corner of the bar in Budapest, Pittsburgh, Binghamton—in the rusting cities in the rusting places where we leaned against the wall, in the smoky haze of bar smoke and breath, in the rooms at the top of the twisting stairs where we slept and fucked in the lullaby of the radiator's hiss. What we keep is small change in a child's palm. What we keep is our tongues clucked in our cheeks. I sip glasses of harsh gold, mash my teeth, my hand reaching for that dress you wore, like a factory girl on a Friday after she's quit on the last day of summer. What keeps us from worms is this tough, rough-handed kiss. To swing against slag, the purple hills of mid-autumn outside the city of bridges and blue sun, the distant tintinnabulations of church bells, blur of twilight, candles lit by widows in the windows of old farmhouses. Falling into the full grapevines along the lake, the fields our hands furrowed. In the cluttered cupboards where we keep what comes. Someone turns out the kitchen light, walks through the rooms we once rented, walks away from the unraveling rain. The dime-thin dust on the windowsills where with fingers we traced our names.

In the Mouth of Anyone You

All these blessings in the air today, the house of remember her.

The house of a favorite mug of tea. Transcendence,

that simple, as the sound of traffic, all the living rushing off to wage.

And She: a child, a little regretful, together the too of us cooing on the
      backyard swing.

She this earth, dug with a spade, the spring planting. What the heart

opens, forgets, we climb a spiral fire escape the sky calls

grace, lifting us against the clouds, uncaged, grasping—

for what is meant by the unpredictable exchange. Between two

a dozen luminescent prayers

in the city of glass, I write you Blue. I write you a language

of snow-covered winter coats, falling loose. We said

things well, we said, love Capitalized. Our own country

written on blue envelopes, folded like a paper crane.

This sky is ours. Without fear, the planets sound

all these blessings, in the house where we slept,

what would have meant is to follow, of being asked

to never disappear—

Hinges

Blur, head-scarf, mollusks, to arrive at last, passed the woman next door watering her azaleas, in a small flat at dusk, and you turn, head strafed with summer sweat, past the blur of children running outside, in the light nearly the color of blush, when you were young, naïve, foolish, all the Victorian threads.

How does it happen, to not see it, to not hear the birds in the eaves' troughs singing under the sound of workers bending to hammer the black tiles onto the synagogue roof, the mailwoman with her large package for you, the light. Never underestimate the light of this arrival, this gleaming glare. And you are there, in the kitchen with water steaming and your damp hair, and the hands that circle your hips and you are dancing in the country named for desire, named tender freedom, a neighborhood named sauerkraut. What's there is what floats in the soup above what drowns, naked and lit. The body without a defense. For all fences cannot exist, the wire, barbed and coiled that you gathered, the tall wooden slates hiding the lot where nothing grows, suddenly blossoms, everywhere. When you turn on the crowded street as if the air parts, we've all seen it: Cinemascope. A soundtrack of opera, Toscanini. Vivaldi in spring. On the eve of the long apparition of certain. Near immanent cities of not this time. At the train station, half asleep, a name flutters like a flute on the loudspeaker, ahead a half century of bliss. The watch stops, the eyes look up. The mollusked world pulls apart, a pearl that swings swings on broken hinges.

After the Election

what book is opened what hand-drawn pictures of saints what humble shrouds ruby'd in the earth's flooded grief there in dog-hearted exile let the roses sweep exhausted on the ground at the feet of the strikers crying for bread in the poor drizzle against factory windows someone is sewing the map of the world of what should be human with sound in the rooms of bare bulbs in the unkempt child's hair in the mother's gold comb in the music of trucks in the calling and the kiss like little trumpets there is a love that is thick as the breath from loaves cooking in a crowded kitchen where the amputees bow their heads to read the map that stops us from lying a new life will enter like a long walk through the state of ruin to love this city will celebrate 6:32 P.M. a boy raises his bicycle in the city of what could be what should be he unrolls a map a red bicycle with silver rims and he rides past cathedrals Italian-restaurants bodegas wheelchair-races greenhouses cookie shops t'ai chi ballets in the parks where the jails have been turned into print shops beauty parlors bakeries breathe the warm bread on the kitchen table we have spread the map run our fingers over the avenues of lentils the boulevards of sangria eggplant arroz chutney couscous la conga in a bakery box in a blueberry muffin in the breaking in the bowing in a bottle of milk in the newspaper where the pages are blank and we lift our crayons with our new bodies where we draw like umbilical cords like kite strings the lines that lead into the never known mispronouncing the new words no one has yet to define this new gospel crossing the last eclipse this cartography we claim toward a new refuge this new passage rising into these houses of bread inside you.

Eating Violins

Can you hear the strings
  as she chews on the frets?
To sing her name like a fish
  through albatross oceans, like
Chinese galleons sailing
  in the fifteenth century
to proclaim *The Excellence*
  of the Dynasty, the fireworks,
the porcelain, the Shanghai
  poem, yes like all those sailors
who traded blue bowls
  on the coast of East Africa,
though our names may cease
  your name will become salt, sails,
sequins, starfish.
  You are the Southern Cross,
Andromeda over the Himalayas.
  In the weary shade of a waitress's hands
at a diner counter in San Antonio
  long past midnight, I will stutter
You are love's lost letters,
  You are this tattoo: black
sun burn, good weather.
  With your name we will transform all sobbing
into high-fives, food stamps will become
  broken bread, fish that leap into the palms,
you are the guitar chord that courses through traffic
  changing curses
to kisses, upturned eyes becoming
  the clouds transforming themselves
into egrets, blue herons, fire engines
  whose sirens sing from Palo Alto
to Alcatraz, Paris to Bombay,
  to the shade of the Great Pyramid

where we spread our arms to utter *take me*
      without anger, you who are not saint
but so human, who did not give up
      for what the world could not give, I will spend
the last coin in my pocket
      to give to a boy in Manila
into his fist is where the revolution begins,
      in the holy wings of the dragonfly,
in the spiders you feared,
      in their miraculous webs dripping
with rainwater, in the factories
      of teeth and crutches,
let us fix the bottled ships
      of Pablo Neruda, every bus stop, train station,
in the nervous stutter of the lawyer
      I sit beside as the plane begins to rise
over parapets and ghettos whose light
      lights the night, we shall carry you like Ezekiel,
Zapatista, Emma Goldman, funky as Sly
      on the bass, trancing with Bedouins
in the sands of Marrakech, we shall spill ouzo
      off the coast of Salamanca, work in the factories
that hammer the icons of Mary,
      paint her downturned lids, and I will
utter *she is you* in this blue dress,
      bought for a few dollars by a widow
who kneels in the hushed votive light,
      Let all anger become forgiveness,
grant us a few minutes to pause
      between shifts, let our lips
become shackled with your kisses.
      I will tell the cab driver in Denver
She is a birch tree brilliant
      in winter. And for the prisoner, I will say
She is a little girl eating a violin.

Notes

"Your Voice After Desnos": The line "your voice is a locked puppet" riffs the title to Turkish poet Ali Yuce's *Voice, Lock, Puppet,* trans. Gerry LaFemina and Sinan Topruk.

"The Long Waiting": The form of this piece is called a "collapsed canzone"—a traditional canzone collapsed into a prose poem.

"Canzone Sprayed with Graffiti" is a conceptual form, based on the traditional canzone with an interwoven theme/image of visual arts, dance, music, text, and love varied instead of an end word (repeton). The italicized lines are taken from poems by Alla and Marina Meroshnik, Ukranian-American high-school students from Erie, Pennsylvania.

"Dear Pistachio" was written after reading the quote from French theorist Hélène Cixous: "In love relationships we have a tendency to give each other animal names. But we don't call each other vegetables as often. It is more difficult to elaborate upon our vegetable side and our identification with vegetables... Our body is the place of this questioning. And what about the flower part in our body?"

"Pas de Deux" was written after a quote by John Yau: "David Lehman and I do a little dance." All capitalized phrases are actual names of dance forms.

"Call Out" was generated partly from the quote by legendary jazz drummer Max Roach: "The thing that frightened people about hip hop was that they heard people enjoying rhythm for rhythm's sake."

"The Day Biggie Smalls Died": Frank White refers to Christopher Walken's character from the movie *The King of New York.* Biggie often claimed be was "the Black Frank White." "Five songs he never wrote down" refers to the claim that he was carrying five new songs he was writing in his head and was set to record right before he was shot.

"Oberek": The Oberek is a form I invented based on the three-beat Polka Waltz. The Oberek uses as its base a three-beat foot: unstress, stress, stress. Often in process though this form was let loose to let the poem find its final form. This is similar to honky-style polka, which often moves into an improvised form and rhythm.

"My Father's Fro in the Mode of Romare Bearden": *Marvins* refers to Marvin Gaye. Legba is a Yoruban god. Bootsy Collins was bass player for the legendary funk band The Parliament. Orishas are a kind of Yoruban spirit or angel. Dejembe is an African drum. Walt Frazier was a flamboyant NBA point guard in the late 1960s and early 70s. Amadou Diallo was an African immigrant mistakenly shot (51 times) by New York City police officers as he reached for his passport.

"Oberek for Etheridge Knight": Etheridge Knight was a great American and African-American poet. A former prisoner, he wrestled with drug addiction throughout his lifetime until his death in 1991.

"Kowalski: A Historiography": Ady refers to Endre Ady (1877–1919), great Hungarian journalist, poet, and cultural figure. The quotes from "Suzanne" are derived from a chance encounter in Budapest with a Holocaust survivor at Saint Stephen's cathedral. The form of this piece is another "collapsed canzone."

"Eating Violins" is for the great American political activist and folk singer Jolie Rickman, who was a leader in the Stop the School of Americas movement. She died of cancer at the age of 33 in 2004.

Acknowledgments

Great thanks to the editors of the following print, electronic, and audio publications:

Antioch Review: "Oberek for Etheridge Knight";
Bitter Oleander: "Your Voice After Desnos";
Caketrain: "Pas de Deux";
Cimmaron Review: "Kowalski: A Historiography";
Conduit: "In This Very Room";
CutThroat: "Black Earth";
Double Room: "Hinges";
88: "Narrative I Don't Know How to Spell";
Harpur Palate: "After the Election," "The Dark Soul of the Accordion," "What We Keep";
Gargoyle: "Oberek";
Jubilat: "All You Ask for Is Longing";
Lake Affect: "In the Mouth of Anyone You";
The Minnesota Review: "The Sentence";
The New York Quarterly: "Hades";
Quarter After Eight: "Call Out";
Pleiades: "Brief Blues";
Phoebe: "Galicia";
Poet Lore: "On the Heroic Ledge";
Poetry East: "Canzone Sprayed with Graffiti," "Dear Pistachio," "Eating Violins";
Rattapallax: "Embraceable You";
Redactions: "Night";
Under Currents (Canada): "The Long Waiting";
Virginia Quarterly Review: "In the Republic of Pantomime";
Word is Bond: "My Father's Fro in the Mode of Romare Bearden."

"After the War" was published in the anthology *POETRY 30* (Mammoth Books, 2005) edited by Daniel Crocker and Gerry LaFemina.

Gratitude to the Atlantic Center for the Arts for a full fellowship and to master teacher John Yau. Thanks to the Pennsylvania Council on the

Arts for Fellowships in 2004 and 2006 that enabled me to live and write, and to Penn State University for a Research Fellowship to Budapest.

Thanks to my editors Peter and Thom and the entire BOA family, to my colleagues at Penn State Erie, to my friends Bill, Chris, Corey, Cody, Gerry, George, Diane, Jeff, Jim, Joe, Justin, Shelly, Matt, Peter, Raleigh, Terrance, and Tom. To Suzanne and John. Thanks to Gabriel, the reason I live. Thanks to every venue where I ever performed.

About the Author

Sean Thomas Dougherty was born in 1965. He is the author or editor of ten books, including the forthcoming experimental novella *The Blue City* (Marick Press) and *Nightshift Belonging to Lorca* (a finalist for the Paterson Poetry Prize). His awards include two Pennsylvania Council on the Arts Fellowships in poetry and a Penn State University Junior Faculty Research Award. Known for his electrifying performances, he has toured extensively across North America and Europe. He received an MFA in poetry from Syracuse University. He lives with his son Gabriel in Erie, Pennsylvania, and teaches in the BFA Program for Creative Writing at Penn State Erie.

BOA Editions, Ltd.
American Poets Continuum Series

Colophon

Broken Hallelujahs, poems by Sean Thomas Dougherty, is set in Baskerville, an electronic version of a font originally designed by John Baskerville (1706–1775) of Birmingham, England, and punchcut by John Handy.

The publication of this book was made possible, in part, by the special support of the following individuals:

Anonymous (6)
Nancy & Alan Cameros
Gwen & Gary Conners
Whitman & Max Conners
Wyn Cooper & Shawna Parker
Susan DeWitt Davie
Peter & Sue Durant
Pete & Bev French
Dane & Judy Gordon
Kip & Deb Hale
Tom Hansen
Robin & Peter Hursh
Archie & Pat Kutz
Stanley D. McKenzie
Daniel M. Meyers
Don & Ellen Parker
Boo Poulin
John Roche
Deborah Ronnen
Gerald Vorrasi
TCA Foundation on behalf of Mid-Town Athletic Club
Thomas R. Ward in memory of Jane Buell Ward
Mike & Pat Wilder
Glenn & Helen William
David Woo

❖